# A Double Act

Other books by the authors in collaboration:

*Airborne Dogs* (Brunswick Hills Press, 1988)
*The Ferrara Poems*, a verse novel (Experimental Art Foundation, 1989)
*The Gutman Variations* (Little Esther, 1993)
*The Wallah Group* (Little Esther, 2001)
*Nutters Without Fetters* (PressPress, 2002)
*Poems of Relative Unlikelihood* (Little Esther, 2005)
*Lucky For Some* (Little Esther, 2012)

# A Double Act

The Selected
Collaborative Poems

## Ken Bolton & John Jenkins

PUNCHER & WATTMANN

First published in 2022
Published by Puncher and Wattmann
PO Box 279
Waratah NSW 2298

https://www.puncherandwattmann.com
web@puncherandwattmann.com

ISBN    9781922571465

Cover design & incidental artwork by Ken Bolton
Typesetting by Morgan Arnett
Printed by Lightning Source International

A catalogue record for this work is available from the National Library of Australia

# Contents

*from*
# Airborne Dogs

# Airborne Dogs

"Great rainbow out there!" said Trigger
"Yes!" Elmo almost yelped, "Makes you think, doesn't it!"
"What?!?" "Makes You Think! Makes *me*
think of one of those little Orphic Cubist paintings
done 'as from the air'—of the Eiffel Tower and Paris!"

"Don't know 'em" Trigger responded, "where we gonna *land?*"
"On that little patch of sand, down there."

"Don't miss, remember, or you'll hear bells chime for days
and days after, boy!" "Cut out that boy stuff" Elmo whined.
They floated through the air.
Trigger bit at his guy-ropes, bit and gnawed,
drifting a little left. "Don't know Paris?"
"Yeh, dunno it." A bird started. (You know the way

a bird 'starts'. Not the way
a novel starts. The way, the way

... The way a cat does if you kick it,
sneaking up on it, slowly, *Kick!* the cat starts, (automatically).
        like that. And
flew past squawking. "No no no—I didn't mean Paris—'Do
you know *Paris?*'—I meant those little Delaunays,
Delaunay did of it." "Of what?" "Of PARIS!"

By this time three more dogs had jumped, and they had touched down,
their parachutes lying sideways, on the ground.

Elmo touched down first. Then Trigger. They sniffed around.

No sign of dogs. Above, white dots descended, the air full of
       growls
(dogs descending). Three dots only. "Houston's woofed it."
"What?" said Elmo. "Woofed it, woofed it, *WOOFED it!!* Are you
*Deaf?!"*

"He has woofed it too, or he'd be here now," said Sharon,
drifting down too. "Maybe he landed on that flat-iron!

And got whisked away!" They'd landed near a train line.
But no train was on it.
"Parachutes Off Here!" barked Diggingest, the last to land.
A soft squashed pyramid of parachute silk
formed, like a flattened omelette, or snow-blind cow-patty...

(Get the picture? Yes, We See.—To quote the old Shangri-las LP).
(Forensic, the fourth to land, always used the royal *We.*)

This is a good spot to talk about the dogs:
Trigger, the leader, a bit Philistine as you've seen, named
after a dog! *not a* horse (another dog named Trigger—who just didn't
       want a dog's name);
then Elmo, a dog's dog, though refined; then Sharon
who used lots of dog slang (like "woofed it" and "I could go a beer")
       to be

in with the crowd; Houston, who missed the Time Hole,
(of which more later—some explanation, description etc, a
       little theory—will be our goal);

Forensic! whose name explains all, and Diggingest
whose name explains nothing, it was just a name after all, had

no meaning really, though it *signified* ("like crazy" as Sharon
        would say): it signified Diggingest, his mother's
        favourite dog.
That's them all then—isn't it? And their mission? To rescue—
another dog! Operating under two names. (He's called

Butch on earth, but Cuddles in New Kennel—where our dogs have
come from.) "Where's this train line lead," said Sharon, "have

You got any clue?" "Clue?" growled Trigger, "I know. It goes
to the Southern Obedience Dog Training School." They all looked
        pained
(at the quoting of this name). Trigger led the way, five dogs
        sniffing,
along the tracks. Meanwhile, back to Houston. Houston missed the
        Time Hole. Woofed it. For these dogs come from
New Kennel, a planet, a parallel world, 10 seconds out of phase
        with our own, and different too in other ways: of interest
        here, the status of humans—like dolphins on Earth, remote,
        few, and thought benign.

"Only a creep would a human bite." (Old New Kennel Saying.)
Would that Cuddles had *equal* rights, down here.

In fact, theirs was a Mission of Equal Rights.
But Houston's woofed it: he's missed the Time Hole and floats
        about in a sort of orbit, with alarm clocks ringing all
        around him,
all out-of-time, with just about Everything
in the Known Universe,
Except itself! Most confusing. All are set for different times
        and most go too fast to read them properly, plus *Ring Ring!*
        Yipe, what a way to be suspended...!

Time for an omelette? Well, how would you know? Meanwhile,
        on Earth—neither New Kennel
or that weird sphere old Houston's stuck in—making their way
        through oceans and oceans of lime green fennel,

Our dogs march, along the train line, and there it is! before them,
        a Canine Stalag.
Where cruel sounds—'Heel! Roll over! Fetch that bone!'—assault
        their ears—first faintly, but louder
As they approach its dull grey walls. It's a prison! Hate 'em.
        It brings out the Shelley in Elmo—
Prisons! Freedom, and all of that! "Shut Up Elmer," Sharon warns
as the dogs sneak closer. Inside, one dog, Cuddles, sits all alone
        just 'a-baying' at the moon! But not, really.

Really he knows it's about that time when the Time Holes
Between the two worlds align: "Maybe this month they will come and
        get me," he thinks and hopes. Big bowls

of boring Pal are placed before him but Cuddles does hardly notice.
        —Off his food? No,
He listens, for the sound. Does he hear it? Does he? "Did you
        hear anything?" says one keeper to the
other. "Nuh." In fact they *nearly* did. They didn't because the
        sound is just too high for human hearing. But Cuddles
        hears it!
A whistle (meaning): "Now! we make the break! Over here!" He's
        ready.
And Forensic, with lightning speed though calmly, digs a tunnel

underneath the wire. Another whistle! Cuddles runs!—Closer—
        then—he's there. Out! "I'm Free!" he barks
"Shuttup," each dog warns. Then, as-a-dog, they turn and run, into the
        dark...

Night. Searchlights flare from the towers, probe the dark after
        them
In the fennel they are safe—where no lights penetrate.
A narrow escape. Cuddles meanwhile tells his story.
Why was he there? A mere fun drop between two worlds! How was
        he to know two worlds could be so different? But they were.
        And he was captured.
Later, back at the site: "Strap on your rockets." They get them
        from underneath the silken omelette thing they left behind
        (parachutes actually).

Ready?! *WOOSH!* Clouds whip past real quickly as they streak into
        the sky
Just as their plane flies by, with magnets on it, on its side, a
        rendezvous, six dogs and a plane, in the sky

Just above New Kennel, and just beside—adjacent to—the Time
        Hole—six dogs, through,
Where There Should Be Seven! Houston's woofed it, though how
        could he know—as they passed through—here was his
        chance
to just grab them and pass through too, dragged back through the Time
        Hole? He couldn't.
And he didn't. Again he's woofed it. Through no fault of his own.
        Poor beggar *ring ring ring* (clocks) whirring round,
stuck in this zone. Timelessly. Or you could say forever,
        if it meant anything. (Einstein explained this, in 1905

see the 'Special Theory', and the 'General Theory', of 1916.) "I
better go back and get poor silly Houston," says Diggingest. "Fly

Me To The Moon" he sings, as he takes off (his little joke), four
        little alarm clocks are strapped to each paw—

Why? An extra joke for Houston! Nothing to do with Einstein (though
        who knows?) Diggingest has
A special strong magnetron up his sleeve, as he rockets
To the Edge of Time still whistling. "Fly me to the
MOOOOOON" yowls Houston as Diggingest whips past

And CLUNK! their magnets lock — and Clunk again —
As they are thrown, back through the Time Hole and stick onto the plane
        again,

All safe. Their plane flying (happily) back to New Kennel to touch
        down, where dogs are free.
That place of which all dogs dream, when sometimes they just seem
        to be sitting by the fire. One of them twitches! Perhaps
        he dreams of that zone where you woof it? Who knows?

Remember this and treat dogs fairly. Why not? They never hurt *you!*

*(This poem was brought to you by the RSPCA, as part of some
Community Project.)*

# September the 5th

What's this one about,
do you think

Does it mean,
asymmetrical <u>things?</u>

There are <u>things</u> that are asymmetrical,
and you use them—to judge by,

**You know that I have no natural style of my own?**
**It's true !!**

**I'm like water—odorless and colorless**
**It's true**

**and tasteless**
**I become coloured by my environment, by**
**anything I come in contact with**

**It's true—this is how I experience myself.**

Really?

What do you think they mean by this?


**No No No No No No No! Not asymmetrical things—
the body's own asymmetry!**


The body's own—the body uses *it* to judge by?


like the shape of your nose ?!


**Yeah. Well, no, the brain's hemispheres.**


Right.

## "SINK OR SWIM?"

## "SWIM! SWIM!"

# Magnum Opii

I thought I saw Stella Stevens on
TV the other day. But it wasn't.


No?
Yeah.


You know where she was born,
Hot Coffee!


Yeah?
Yeah, the other day I thought I nearly had a


flat tyre.
Nearly had one?


Nearly *thought* I had one


Yeah?
Yeah.


Hot Coffee?


Yep.

# Lamenting the Flipper

A good dentist overlooks petulance
As in the assertion "I know that!"
Shouted from the Chair, and merely nods, "hrumph", or repeats "They'll
Have to Go."
Or mumbles "Now is the time,"
As he begins to extract all your teeth.
WHY?
Think about it. Try this: take a useful
Length of dental floss
And instruct the dentist To leave, while you
'Rinse'.
When you're alone, start 'relating'
To your teeth,
Use the dental floss as you do,
Does your mouth feel 'gummy'? If not, perhaps you
Have made a mistake. Perhaps you shouldn't even be there! But
Suddenly, there is a lot of screaming from within
"The blanks silence collapse into".
These, you don't often hear, but there you are: and you do (do hear them).
It's as if the pain were so intense, that it obliterated
(Or collapsed together) all distinctions between subject and
Object, in a blast of pure subjectivity.
Ripping the doors from the waiting room and surgery. Or it's
As if the brain were an island, and you've stubbed your foot,
Coming up the sand, to retrieve a flipper, that the waves are carrying
Fast away. Just as the anaesthetic starts working.
But was this your flipper, or the dentist's, *your* scream
Or his, or perhaps only the scream of another patient, or one heard on
Television, or the radio in the surgery. Yes, not even
An authentic scream,

The scream of an actor. This last thought is depressing. This thought
*Is very* depressing. After all,
They're your teeth. But, now,
Isn't that a song? "Coming
Up The Sand"? Or something *like* that?

Perhaps it was the wind in the palm tree,
Where now you lean, watching the flipper float out to sunset. You have
No idea. And no idea is perilously close to 'the idea of nothing',
And
An idea that goes unspoken
Yet terrifies *millions,*
As the idea of nothingness has, is a dangerous idea. It's like the
Idea of eternity. It takes *forever* to think about. And not only
Terrifying, but irritating. Well, these are the sort of things you
Think,
As you shrug, *lamenting the flipper,* your favourite flipper, which
Has sunk beneath
The waves, leaving just a thread of bubbles. Perhaps you are
Just tired, after all *it's been a hard day.* You were *partial* to your
Teeth. *And* you
"May have a fever"!

# In Ferrara

Sunlight dried the last small patches of moisture
on the table top.  Karl wondered if
it was wine,
or dew,
from the night before.
He pushed his cuticles back
with a corner of the menu.  Motor scooters
went by, then a car.
Everything seemed pleasantly European, the
best part of being in Europe, out doors, at
a table.  He moved under
the awning.  As yet only a few people presented themselves
to the morning glare.  His suit,
despite his being a big man, hung loosely on his frame
as Karl bided his time, and made
every effort to keep his mind blank.
Karl had a sort of large round face,
with widely spaced brown eyes,
the sort women found attractive.  His
face was slightly red,
though he hadn't walked far to the café.
His were the sort of looks
that seemed ripe to fade
though they never had.  There
was something vaguely raffish
and un-German about
him, that was not to be
attributed, either, to half a
life in Australia, where
he bought for a chain of bonbonniere.

He made this trip often,
visiting glass factories and warehouses
between here and Venice, and
as far north as Southern Germany.
All his life, things had gone
right for Karl. The result
being, strangely enough, a slight
lack of confidence and a self-doubting air.
He had never struggled, and
his success did not surprise him,
but it confirmed nothing. He glanced
at his watch with some abstraction.
He was a handsome man
and when in doubt, as he was so often,
given to pose. The chair beside him
moved. "Giselle, hello." Giselle sat
down. "Good morning Karl." And
she looked down the plaza,
squinting into the shadows for
the others: "Have you ordered?"
"No. Well, I think so. The waitress
doesn't seem to have noticed."
Giselle called to the waitress: "Praego,
Signora!" And, gaining her attention,
"Per favore, duo café." Giselle
scratched her nose and flicked out a
cigarette which she then placed carefully
by the packet, not lighting it.
They were at ease and
Karl chose not to notice, remarking
instead on the Alitalia flight over
the distant conifers, growing on the low
hills that surrounded Ferrara—the contrast

of modernity and ancient towers.
Giselle wore a tight black dress,
and dark glasses which she had removed.
Her nose was finely chiseled,
and fluted, almost pinched, yet beautiful.
Giselle generally was attractive,
and made small flourishes with her hands.
She acknowledged the arrival of
their coffees for herself and Karl
in a way that had become habitual.
She worked as a tour guide, and
her work had bred her
manner and talents. Giselle
worked privately, for well-off tourists.
She was mildly bored with her job
but did not find it irksome.
She looked up as Greg
arrived, and so did Karl. Though they
had spoken on the telephone
this was the first time they had met.
Karl knew Greg from Sydney.
"Giselle, Greg." "Hello." "Greg, Giselle."
"Hello, I spoke to you earlier. Yesterday."
"I know." Her voice trailed off. "How's
it going with your arrangements?" Karl asked. "You've
found a hotel?" Greg put a
map on the table and answered
in the affirmative. "Which one," asked Giselle.
Greg looked up from the map. "The Grand...
The Grandé," and went on, "They're not very helpful.
I was trying to find an all-night pharmacia."
Roberto arrived and called for the waiter.
He gave his order standing up, then sat down.

Giselle introduced Roberto to Greg,
and the others re-ordered. Roberto
exercised an immediate presence,
to which Giselle responded, as did
Greg and Karl. There was about Roberto
an air of some risk,
against which a physical substantiality
gave assurance. Despite the
similarity of size, Roberto seemed
larger, to take up more room, than Karl.
Roberto may have been slightly younger,
though he seemed more mature and far
more active in some indefinable way—
that was something to do with gesture,
the carriage of his head, and even his clothes.
Karl also wore glasses and spoke
with some hesitation. Roberto was dark
where the other was fair. And his business
career had been more volatile. At
present, as the others understood,
he presided over the liquidation
of a marble quarry
from a deceased estate, clearly
at some temporary benefit to himself.
They drank their coffee. Roberto
spoke briefly to Greg. Old friends
from Sydney—though Giselle, who
had been longest away, had
not previously met Greg. With the exception
of Greg all were well-travelled and
at ease with each other. Hitherto,
he had not ventured from Australia.
His presence here was much less

business than the others', though it was
presenting him with the most difficulty.
He spoke vaguely, addressing Karl
and Roberto. "Is there some way of
going from my hotel to the old
section of town? Is it walking distance?"
At this point there was a confused clatter
and the sounding of a high-pitched horn.
They looked around just in time
to see a Vespa scooter describe
an uncertain path across the
cobblestones towards them
and collapse a mere few metres away.
At first none stood. The embarrassed rider,
a young woman, looked to her
slightly buckled machine, and to the bus
that had forced her from her path.
As the girl rubbed dirt
from her knee, Giselle took her
by the arm and led her to
the other three. "Are
you hurt?" they asked. "What happened?"
"I think the bus did not see." "You
speak English?" responded Karl. "Mm, Yes.
I go to school in England." Giselle gave her a chair.
"We are Karl, Robert, and Greg," indicating
each, "And I am Giselle." "I am
Carla Merighi." Greg went
to pull the scooter upright
and parked it by the fountain.
As he returned Carla was saying
"I live just near here. Thank
you, you are very kind." "You

are alright?" "*You must be very certain,*" Karl admonished.

"Could I have a glass of water?"

# A Mood

"Let's go with the mood, if this is a mood really
& not just a way of proving
you can stay up late and not watch television."

Your glass gets empty
so you fill it up.

You fill it up
and it gets empty. How bout that?

I like your hat.

Yeah.

Outside, there are clouds under the moon
but you can't see them
so what's that to you?
(It's night.)
(Reason you can't see em.)
The window
is too far
from your hand
to open.
It sort of
hangs there
in the air anyway
and falls slowly,
later, around a glass
(that somebody filled)
and you drink it. You

think: who cares? And
that's a mood. Or

something like it. Phew!
as Slim himself
might have said—or one of them other guys
Warren Oates or someone —
as you take off your hat,
and are glad,
you're not bald.
Don't laugh, it happens.
And you put the hat down,
over your drink, and open the window.
(Now you're in an entirely new mood.)
And There Are!
(Clouds out there)
under the moon, a
bald moon. And there are televisions on

all along the street

and no one's watching them,
except me,
breathing, one breath at a time
but a little heavier than I used to.
Clouds, one by one, under the moon
that the wind is blowing to bits.

# The Coffee of Kings

aeolian heart    a cooking thing

the red snow    Country & Western food

Randolf Stow    something to do with what Michael was talking about

and Randolf Scott!    what's another area

"Art Talk Suite"    cell structure

Did you like that too?    money flow

Brokenhearted    seen Bill?

mysterious money  a wall of bricks

funny funds  Michael buys a rubber knife

the burnt edge of that test tube  *I seed* a rubber brick

Cliff Richard granite granules    something that's fantastic

the film star    a theoretical 'thing'

Baby you're a sight for sore eyes  part of an anatomy

'Bushwhacked'    fix that fence  Fabulous  a fence fixed beautiful

knee deep in clover  how I see things

little truffles    fingers *please !*    when the archipelago sank

I notice a little 'thing'

(Charly Brown)

one false moof and I die you!

Atlantis in moonlight

        Says whom

telegraphic    She's so gloriously insincere    codes

brain chemistry  two easy by half  breakfast of champions

The Half That Wasn't There (!)    breakfast for you, too.

I'm famished    studios for rent  I'm halfway not.  permanent and

            casual

Ask not for whom the bell tolls — it tolls for dinner!

the Dan Hicks effect

sweat shone under the quiet lights    a nutter

distant electrons dug out of walls    little models

surface tension        why angoras are fun

the tension of fools     idiot's revenge   What I thought

Kiss me stupid        Quiet, mindless riot         tinkering

                            the

                        perfect past

It's a doggy dog world

al dente    Yes? No? Maybe?   al presto too

not too often    7 years in heaven    rotten diction

Huge dioramas, basted like ice    eat and run     The gift of seizure

eyes front    Don't give *me* that

The big question     I like Ike    Do you think that I should change

A perfect night, sun halo, corona    I don't

OO OO OO, what a little moonlight can do

                      buttons bangles and bows

Billie Holiday

                signification falsification elaboration    those ones

Japanese stamp

             patent pending

a graph buckled in the boardroom    Penelope got crosser

I heard it    the hills looked distant    Dangerous times forestalled

Tashkent in the summer    Hire a frail barque

                     A Dictionary of Places

a frail hired one

             *The* dictionary of places

zoom packed enacts intaglios changes held,    none confession riot

the stock and bric a brac of poetry   little bombs    concatenation

pronounced German   swearing

the coffee of kings    I'll be a dag for you baby

the coffee of kings    full stops and how to stoppem

the very coffee     little bloody finger.

# We Meet Again

"Gun the engine for them Roberto," Karl said.
"I can't find the handbrake—Ah," said Roberto,
handing Giselle her large kid-leather bag. "Here."
"Oh, sorry, I put it there where I thought it
wouldn't be in the way.' Roberto gunned the engine.

In a minute Greg came down and waved.
Giselle leaned forward from the back seat and
blew the horn to hurry him, playfully: "Women
are always in the back seat—
one of us must be allowed in front." "Yes,"
said Carla. "Well I'm big enough to stay."
"We're all big enough to do exactly what we want
Karl," Giselle assured quickly. "You know what
I mean, I'm too big to *fit* back there."
Greg's face appeared smiling at the right
Front door, "Beautiful day!" "You
sit in there," gestured Roberto over his shoulder.
"Yes," Giselle spoke enthusiastically, "I'm sitting
with Robert and Karl, you can share the back
with Carla." Giselle sometimes enjoyed
calling Roberto Robert. When she did
she said it incisively. Greg greeted Carla. "What are
we waiting for—we're all here!?" They all watched,
as four women dressed in black carried washing
across the tiny square in front of them
into Greg's hotel. Washing hung
to dry on many balconies they noticed, much of it
white, moving pleasantly behind
pink and red geraniums, in boxes on the balconies.

"Now we go," Roberto spoke to himself, and shouted—
"Allegro! Now we go!" He blew the horn and the car
drove off, revving wildly. "I haven't seen you
since your accident." "What, all this time
I've been out of town and none of you have been sociable?"
Giselle challenged. "We are most of us busy," said Roberto.
"I am still digging up, ha ha, a buyer for my quarry."
"I also have been away," Carla added. "There you see?"
said Roberto comfortably, humming. "Are you alright?"
Karl asked. "Yes. Fortunately," Carla answered,
"completely recovered—from a little graze on the knee."
"How's the Vespa," Greg asked. "It is not so fortunate,
a mechanic, now, unbuckles the wheel."

The friends were together at Karl's suggestion, taken up
eagerly by Roberto who had organized
the car, and the itinerary. All sat silently for a while
looking forward at the pleasant vista that filed
the windscreen on the drive out of town—a small mountain
looming very large, dotted with small white houses.
Giselle sat between Karl and 'Robert',
Greg and Carla in the rear. "Roberto you
are in a good mood." "Four little coffees and this
fine spring weather. Ah, bella!" he gestured widely
to indicate his feelings. "Also some little
sweet cakes. Mmph!" he paused. "On my balcony
this morning." "What?" "That is where I had them."
"I haven't eaten," said Greg. "You will," said Giselle,
"I have packed some nice things." "Is there something
on the radio?" Karl requested. Roberto flicked it on.
**Born In The USA** blasted forth, at incredible volume.
"No!" screeched Giselle. "It must be the Forces Radio. Those
American soldiers, in Germany—so many bases." "Are

we so near the border?" said Karl. The announcer
calmly spoke in Italian, and led into another song,
something spirited and cheerful, as Roberto turned it down
to a pleasant background. "It can't have been the Forces Radio
—not so loud & so far away." The surroundings were now
more rural. "A Roman ruin," remarked Giselle
of some white stone set back from the road. More of it
straddled the ridge. "There's something on it," Greg
observed, of some lingering frieze work. "Yes,
they decorated everything." "Yes we Romans are still
good at making roads." "You're from Sydney." "Well,
but Roman all the same. *N'est-ce pas?*" he added jokingly.
"It is true, Italian engineers are in demand
all over Europe. Deservedly." "They don't decorate anymore,"
said Carla. "It's coming back, decoration," Giselle
responded. "It is a good thing. We have all had
too much severe architecture," Carla expressed herself,
"I like cities a little more con brio." "It is all new
in Australia," said Greg. "Whoa," Roberto spoke and slowed,
and stopped. Some goats, some with bells, strayed across
the road in front of them. A thin but
constant straggle. The car made small noises
from cooling. They were soothed by the slow clinking of bells.
They waited. "Almost hot," said Giselle, stretching.

"We can go now," Giselle broke the silence.
"Karl—there is the Berio Festival in a fortnight,
at Cologne." "Yes I know," Karl nodded and
turned to Greg. "Are you going?" "Well I was
thinking of it before I got here
—I mean Europe—but I don't know that
I will be able." "The violin works I take it?"
"Yes." "They are diamonds," said Karl, "Little diamonds

of composition." Karl paused, "Two to three minutes,
some, and they make so much work seem unwieldy."
"A real *range* of sounds." "Yes." "For a violin."

> "Chevaliers de la table ronde
> Goutons boire, si le vin est bon
> Goutons boire, oui oui oui
> Goutons boire, non non non
> Goutons boire si le vin est bon"

Roberto sang.
"Stop it Roberto, really!" Giselle reasoned happily.
Roberto continued—

> "S'il est bon, s'il est agréable
> J'en borai jusqu' à mon plaisir
> J'en borai, oui oui oui
> J'en borai, non non non
> J'en borai jusqu' à mon plaisir."

"Roberto, you are driving too fast." "Yes, you
certainly are," Giselle confirmed. To which
Roberto responded, "You and Karl, you are jealous
of my driving: *because,* an Italian and his car,
on these fine Italian roads, a special relationship!
Exhilarating!" "Well, together with your singing
and your terrible accent." "*Accents,*" Carla added.
"They are all authentic!" he shouted. "And *none* of them yours.
You have only been back here five years and it is
pure Rossanno Brazzi. And Maurice Chevalier." "Is
that pure?" "Well, you decide—but let somebody else
at the wheel." "Let Giselle drive," said Karl,
with an effort at weariness. The little blue Lancia

stops, and they change places. "It is ridiculous, all this
room in the back," said Roberto, and lumbered recklessly
in there, with Greg and Carla.
The car began a series of sharp descents and
ascents, with extremely scenic twists and turns. "I love
that word 'scenic'," Greg observed.
                              Soon the car
began to labor as they climbed up a particularly
steep hill. All fell silent. The car slowed
to a crawl as they approached the summit. It stopped
with a hiss of steam. "This is terrible," said Karl.
"I know," agreed Giselle. They waited.
"Rosé?" enquired Roberto. "Well, we could."
They left the car and looked out over the hills,
Not unhappily. "Get the rosé." They moved to a patch of shade
Under a stand of connifers. Roberto returned.
"There is a policeman coming," Giselle exclaimed and ran
back to the car. "Flag him down," cried Carla.
"I'm going to."

"Signora, your car… I do not know. But
there is a little tavern and trattoria just down
the hill. Where you could go. The mechanic is
a friend of mine. I know he can fix anything,
Signora." "Right." "I will help you push the car,"
the policeman added encouragingly. "It would
be good to sit down," heavily Roberto reflected.
They got back in the car, Greg and Karl
and the policeman pushing. The flat of the hill
was but a little distance, and soon the men
had joined the car. The policeman pushed
easily, as the Lancia began to roll, down
the hill. Their arms waved to the policeman

as they bumped downward. He
waved tiredly, watching their descent
and returned to his bike. "I don't see
a garage," Giselle wondered. The foot
of the hill was deeply shady, under a
giant tree, where the road turned. They
drove in silence. Around the corner
was the loveliest little garage. "There it is!"
shouted Carla. The Lancia coughed
past the house's garden, round the side
to the bowsers. The five got out.
Karl spoke to the mechanic as the others
stood aside. The mechanic nodded.
He opened the bonnet with Karl and they talked quietly.
More loudly he spoke, leading Karl to the others
then around the corner, to the side of the house
and a table. "His mother, he says will attend us,"
explained Karl. "We will wait, for lunch?" he asked.
They flopped at the tables and ordered wines and salad
and olives. "Even if we had not broken down,
it is very pleasant here," said Carla. "Yes." "Yes
it is," said Giselle. Karl sipped his frascati,
his face slightly flushed. He moved out of the sun
into the shade that dappled the others. As
they ate, the house's chickens moved, at first tentatively,
among their tables. It was very relaxing.
"Let us do the *eating* part of the picnic here,"
said Karl, "and take the blankets and wine up into
the hills later. We can still see the view."
"If the car works," said Carla. "He says
it will," Karl assured them. "Good idea,"
said Greg. They all assented, suddenly relieved
at the removal of their uncertainty. Roberto fed the chickens.

"Do you want to see me hypnotize one?" Karl addressed
them, staring fixedly at a chicken, very slightly
grinning. "Karl, no!" Giselle insisted. "Mind
against the Chicken!" said Greg, seeming interested.
"Chook chook chook chook chook. Chicky-chick, chick-chick
chick-chick chook. Chooky chooky." The bird moved
irritably away. They ate the bread and cheese and olives.
The garage proprietor appeared, wiping his hands. "Your car
it is fixed I think, signors and sigorinas." "Shall we?"
"Let's go, yes," said Carla, "we must see the hills
before the sun sinks further." They moved to the car.

*

"This would be a good spot," said Giselle. "Yes,"
said Karl approvingly—looking out to their right,
across a rugged but green and softened valley. To
their left, ascending to the top of the hill, was a carpet
of almost uniform flowers blooming, the remains of
a former flower farm. A distant church bell
tolled the early afternoon hour as they got from the car
and spread blankets and a table cloth, some books and baskets.
"This is great," sad Karl. "Yes." "Yes.
Though there are other things to see, before the sun goes down,"
Roberto remarked almost somnolently. He took his
jacket off and scratched his stomach through his T-shirt.

They all sat down.

Greg said, " I sell cameras but I didn't feel like
bringing one with me." "It's a burden,"
Giselle put in, somewhat heavily somewhat lightly,

adding, "to be always putting something between
your perceptions and the world, in the anticipation
of a sort of retrospective memory. Most of your
perceptions are second-hand anyway. Either
you are a moron who doesn't see that, and takes the
picture on reflex or you spend your life worrying,
Is *this* the picture I should take, authentically,
or is it just a picture." "I don't like taking photos either."
"And then you never bother to look at them," she went on, her
     voice
falling through tones heavily. "I don't like lightmeters,
I don't like loading the camera," Roberto offered, as a
codicil. Karl added humorously, "I have an album
full of photos of my thumb." But his remark
fell on silence. "I have only ever thought of it in
abstract, I have never intended owning a camera,"
Carla said. "Here we are, well, anyway," Karl said, "Should
we look at it?" "Okay," said Roberto. "It's beautiful,"
Giselle acquiesced graciously. "Where is this?" said Greg.

They talked a little, sometimes in no tones,
sometimes laughing. They relaxed and talked and drank.
"I'm going up the hill. To be among the flowers."
Karl paused. And laughed, "Forgive me, I'm a
German." "Caspar David Friedrich," Roberto commented
to Giselle. Giselle played with the grass.
"Sometimes you don't like to think too hard, Roberto."
"Who does?" "No. I mean you." "What? What
have I done?" Roberto grunted. "Fill my glass
you crazy fool," he said. Giselle laughed
and filled it. Karl came down the hill. "Flowers!"
said Karl, holding a bunch of them, but putting them
down carelessly. "I think I'll have a look at

the valley," said Giselle, and moved off to the verge
that afforded, now, a darkening, heightened
view of the valley, streaked with light and
dark greens, the last of the sun picking out
the little white bits of rock that dotted the hill,
and darker boulders and hedges, the sky a brilliant
lowering tide of pigment threatening meaning. "It
is very operatic," she heard Roberto say to Karl.
She heard Karl laugh. Roberto rose up to join
her. "Where are the others?" called Karl.
"Down there actually," said Giselle. "What are
they doing." "They're making love," she observed.
"Really!?" "They are too," said Karl. "How romantic,"
called Roberto, beside Giselle. "It looks like a
liberated *Baci* box," Karl smiled as he joined them.

*

Giselle poured a drink, which Roberto handed him. Time
moved slowly. After a time Roberto remarked,
"Even with friends we can still be surprising." "Not
with me you can't," Giselle snuffled in her glass.
"With old friends we can still be surprising. But not *for* them.
Or not *with* them," Karl pronounced in a low tone
bleached of emotion. Roberto laughed.

* * *

Carla and Greg came over the hill. "Ah," Karl remarked.
"Time to go?" Roberto suggested to them.
They packed and walked slowly to the car. The

car was warm from the afternoon sunshine.
"One more stop to go," reminded Roberto. "Where's
that?" asked Carla. "Ho ho, my surprise." He
put the car in gear. They rocked back and
forth as the little Lancia chugged down the hills
to the road below. They drove in silence, conscious
of the rosy glow of approaching sunset. They
rounded the corner to a strange view, stark and romantic.
"This looks like a quarry," said Greg. Roberto nodded
a little and giggled. "O Roberto!" Giselle shouted.
"Good God," spoke Karl parenthetically.
"Roberto this is *your* quarry. It's lovely. But you
can't expect us to *buy* it!" "You never know,
I would manage it for you," said Roberto,
mocking half-heartedness. "You can't blame me for trying."
"It is beautiful," breathed Carla. "Yes, though I'm not
in the market for a quarry!" Greg threw
his head back and laughed. "Enjoy," said Roberto,
Italianately. They looked at the quarry. "It is
time to go," said Roberto after a while, "I have
No buyers." "It's time," said Carla.

# Dumb

All information aspires to the condition of solipsism.
As in the assertion "I know that,"
a field trip to the 'deep exterior', where we are left
now this is true
surveying the economic trace,
say. Why,
we are 'the Condition of Fictions'—
think about it. Try this: take a useful length of dental floss
and instruct
or impress on your mind
how to experience yourself as an absence.
Use the dental floss as you do. It is
intended to subvert
a kind of psychic inertia—only you don't *know*. Except I told you.
The blanks silence collapses into
you won't even hear. (Concentrating on your teeth.)
*On* your voyage to the centre brain—
a little like a trip inland, on an island—*a little* island,
      one tree, one coconut—(Island as in the sense of No 'man' is one,
      No woman either) but
*without an irritated dermatology of sense.*
Well, *this* happens! There you are,
on the stern of great classic thoughts.
"Whoever had an original idea in the bathroom!" An unfair thought,
yet ditto history
—unfair because, well, Einstein did we know, and the great brains
that thought all these zeitgeists up
hardly knew *where* they were. (At the time.) Now, have you kept
      your dental floss?

It was only a recording device!

The way it happened with Einstein, he raced to the clinic, on his
        daughter's bike—how... well, how loveable I guess.
And they said—now this is history—"What's that in your pocket?"
Besides
not only did the dental floss tell him where he'd had the
        idea (bathroom),
but also, possibly, how he'd got it! (dental floss). *And*
we don't know what this *means* anymore!
We have forgotten what I will tell you now
"**BORN** in the USA! **Born** in the USA!"

# The Gutman Variations

"I distrust a close-mouthed man, sir.
He generally picks the wrong time to talk
and says the wrong things.
Talking's something you can't do judiciously,
unless you keep in practice.
Now, sir, we'll talk if you like. I'll tell
you right out, I'm a man who likes to talk
to a man who likes to talk."

—Caspar Gutman (Sidney Greenstreet) in *The Maltese Falcon*

Pay sir? The *Batchelors From Prague* sir?
Why—have they *brought the bird?*
That is the only reason I would pay sir—
to acquire the bird and bank it.

Tell me the bird is unreal sir? It's
my Desire. I have held the bird sir
for just moments. Encrusted
with diamonds from beak to claw.
I held it against my chest. I felt it.
Tell me, *Real* or *Imaginary?* It
was real to me sir!

To have the bird
is to bank sir.
And I mean to have the bird sir, and bank it.

I don't mind telling you sir
once I get my pinkies on the bird sir
I won't give a fig for Lacan I can tell you.

The bird sir, the bird is all sir.

Real? or Imaginary?

As Lacan's Mother used to say sir, and I quote to you exactly,

*"Jacques, Jacques,* as long *as you are happy!"*

I will be happy when I have the bird.

Think? About anything else sir?
Sir, my mind is a sort of permanent aviary sir,
an empty cage for the bird. I change the water daily,
I fill the cage with furniture and I move it around.
For the bird sir. *Cheap* furniture and avian toys sir,
for I mean to make a profit.




Tell me it is a little bit of my displaced ego sir
and I will tell you you are a fool. I have seen that bird
used as a club in the hands of desperate men in gambling rooms
        in Cairo
and later in Budapest and Madrid.
I have seen it thrown from a four storey building
and crash through the roof of a moving train below sir.
You say the bird is the site of inexpressible ideas
that crowd around me at night. I tell you,
there are no ideas that are inexpressible. All ideas
are expressible by the bird sir. I have a picture of
        the bird sir
that I picked from the pocket of a dead man in
        Istanbul. But you think I am content
with that? It is the bird that I want sir.

*Fort Da is* neither here nor there sir—to me.
He threw his cotton reel too often from the cot sir,
too often entirely. If he had a cotton reel sir
he had it. If he threw it, he threw it. If I had
        the bird sir
I would not throw it away, I would put it on the counter
and say bank that.
No sir—throw it away?—I don't like that sir,
don't like that at all.

Sadly, sir—though I tell you, *I do not care!*—
the Law comes between me sir, and my desire
for the bird.

Yes, sir. I eat duck and chicken sir,
geese, all manner of fowl sir—
to develop an affinity with the bird. Sir,
one must make oneself attractive to the bird sir.
The bird is wealth sir, and as one must trade
one's way out of debt sir, so in this way I become
more like the bird sir. And happy to do it.

Have you any conception of the worth
of the bird?

Sometimes I think sir
*I am* the bird. But I take a walk,
and sing.
*"Just a closer walk with thee."*
And I look around—I am alone.  I am
not the bird.

Lacan takes the mirror image as the model
of the ego.
The 'I' can shift and change places sir
just as the bird can change places. They tell me
I confuse the bird with myself sir. The bird
and I are different, different entirely! I cannot
            bank myself sir
but I can bank the bird!
                        I am 292 pounds
and six feet two inches high sir. The bird is two foot high
and encrusted with diamonds. I ask you sir *are these
subtle differences?* They are not subtle to me sir.
I will have it, I will have the bird!

Frankly, I want that bird.

The meanings and legends that surround the bird
sir are a means to the bird a nimbus
that hovers about it. When I gain the bird
I will say, "Lights out" sir, and come morning
I will be at the door of a bank in Switzerland.
With the bird sir.

I would have that bird!

Assuredly the bird is not I sir—
although it is shifty.


        Have you any conception
        of the *worth* of that bird sir?
        Sir, a sight of that bird is something
        one gives a lifetime to see.


And I have given a whole lifetime, sir.
And I mean to see it again sir.

See it, grab it, *and* bank it.

We take the bird sir to be the mirror and
the repository of my object and my desire sir.
Sir, *the bird mirrors nothing!* It is encrusted
with diamonds and made of gold sir and sheathed in lead.
It is a valuable *object.* Which I mean to bank.

Lacan's Human Subject sir is not a divided self
that in a different society could be made whole sir,
but a self which is only
*actually* and *necessarily* created
within *a split!* a being that can only conceptualize itself
when it is mirrored back in the desire of another.
Do you think sir that I imagine the bird desires *me!*
Poppycock.
Unfortunately, the bird gives not a fig. I have been
in many different societies sir — Melanesian, Europe,
the Near East, the sub continent, northern and tropical
Africa. *And in each of these* I desired the bird.

The 'I' is a shifter
& I mean to shift the bird, shift it to where it is mine.

'Mediated by language'? But as Gertrude Stein
once said to me sir, "Bird is
the word." And I agree with her entirely.
My word.

Assuredly the bird is not I sir—
although it is shifty.

I admire a man who can talk frankly about the bird sir.

Do you imagine
the bird desires *me?* Entirely
not. The bird is indifferent.
The bird is a bird sir. And
I mean to have it.




I do not mean to be enjoined with the subject sir,
or the object—I mean to bank it. The Other
appears to hold the truth of the subject sir
and the power to make good its loss. While it is true
I have incurred certain losses in my search
for the bird sir, they will be more than adequately
          compensated—*when I have the bird.*

Do you imagine that I confuse
the desire of others with
my desire for the bird?
Not for a moment sir, not
a bit of it.

There is only one bird sir, and I mean to *have* it.

Identity and wholeness remain at the level
of fantasy sir. Do they imagine sir
that were I to bank the bird I would bank the *Other,*
that I would somehow be complete, so expanded
as to include within myself sir, encompass, all
that I can imagine? We shall stop the circulation of
        language
when we have the bird sir and we shall certainly stop the
        circulation
of the bird!

*from*
The Wallah Group

# Keeping it All Together

"The journey of a thousand leagues
begins with a single footstep," said Mao
& I'm tapping my foot in time, paying
more respect to the impact
than to reverberations

which shake dust out of the floor

which falls on the heads of those below
because this is the second floor, and one man's
        floor
is *another man's ceiling,*
such as it is in these built-up times.

Maybe he is tapping his foot, too.
No dust falls on the man below—
no guilt, *sure!* But no reverberation.
And each of us is marking time. His &
mine. His in his room

& mine in mine. (Mine
in his room, too, which must be irritating.)
If the song's worth singing
then we all should listen.
But if there is too much echo

no one can hear. Much. It makes sense.
And that's why "the beat goes on" &
everyone goes along with it. You, me,
& the man downstairs, whom
I think is listening.

# Hooning About

So you go left
& there's another road, & there's lights, right?
on *another* corner... *Fuck em!* If I had
wheels, I'd be a *car* : I'd be *good* at it!
I'd have the wheels, see, & I know where the lights are
                              already,
cause I *live* round here!


# (A Line From Ted Berrigan) Inheritance

There's a badge my old dad has
  —he wears it on his beanie!  A tornado-proof
      vest
he'd've needed in the navy.  "It now
    all mine is."


# A Socialist Japan

A fine rain anoints the canal machinery
as I ride my bike over the little bridge to
    Social Security.

# Three
## 'Poems of Relative Unlikelihood' and One Other

## #1  Fat Wallah

Happy to be silly in the long
twilight hours.  The faded sleeve
passes, and the girl with
a lover weeping at her arm.

Traffic flows or stops.

*

You drag that sleeve with some effort
to your brow, and over it,
or mop some aspect of what can only be called
your visage—in this diction
it can only be called that—

and imagine you are become a cloud.

*

Do you remember when we took the
long way home, and talked for hours?
Home late, hours lost
and nothing to show.  Well, nothing
you can see, but it stays with

you all the same, and can come
back years later, recalling that the
moment was a beautiful distraction,
the gesture perfect for shielding your
eyes from the abrasive dust, sights
that can only distract.

*

Though distraction was somehow the point.

*

The girl disappears.

It's funny, to be an extraordinary fat
young Englishman
on a balcony, in a bazaar,
in a foreign land—
a land made unapproachable by various
sorts of cultural commentary
that are anathema to how I feel now
so we will forget about them—funny,
but also noble.

*

My mind is made up, like a bed
or a story. The balcony requires
a beautiful maroon and blue
to illuminate the calendar. Breasts are attractive
because they are made that way,
outlined against silk and the seasons.

*

Admittedly I cannot tell
how big her breasts are—she is
a tiny figure, down there in the bazaar.


The theatre fills and empties,
and the strangers passing in the
street seem entirely familiar.
You catch their eyes or don't,
and they surprise you with their
refusal to comprehend. They are
walking home, together or alone,
as the day demands. And
this is perfect.

                    Only I
am not demanded by the day,
and see its perfection. I attribute it,
a kind of nutty Caesar
of the aesthetic,
and attribute it

only to satisfy my need.

A thought which makes me weep.

*

Lost it. And now I am truly
above and overlooking. I sigh, on
my balcony— and the street recedes

like air about my shoulders as
I turn back to the illuminated
interior. The single chair, the
humming moment, and change my clothes
and go downstairs, whistling.

# #2  In My Yard

I know nothing very clearly—
but with a manifesto resembling
"Fuck that, but"—
non specific, transportable, *transposable,*
to any scheme of reality that seems about
to close in on one—
I move sharply between phenomena.

Well, I invite your use of this device.

So we'll leave that open.  And if we leave
it open enough, everything will flood in,
the night and the day, and fill up all
the available spaces.

      I go outside—
and turn on the sprinkler.  Then,
I go around to the other side,
to the other garden, and pick up the hose.
This is what I love.  I seem to see mostly
almost what I am not looking at.

The eye is an airbrush, coloring in
the real, a circulation of attention,
as the grass grows under my
feet, because it is well-watered,

And I water it, a thousand miles away.

I know *'so much'* very clearly,
and nothing at all—or nothing I can grasp.
But grasping it—what is that?

# #3  Commercial Traveller


When you're in the train, alone
with anticipation and the evening
shuffle, you check that everything
works.  The brain, your body,
little cubes of soap in thin paper.
You have done this before.  And will
do it again.  It has something to do
with the way the weather unfolds.
Or you go out to buy new shoes, full
of optimism that everyone says
will help.


"Latitudes of irony"—take that phrase.
Why is it never longitudes?  Does
longitude describe nothing?


"Pour une peuple corpulent,
*non!*"
                    Why is it
the French are so smart?
I get none of this.


Soon I will get off my train.


                    *


"I only asked!" (that is my attitude).


                    *

Honesty is the best policy, it's what
thrills or hurts.

     Here is my ticket. "Take this,
you bastard." I say that
merely under my breath. In fact—
*though who can say it?*—
I like the look of this nut.

      *

I once walked to the top of
a tall tower and looked out at
all the birds, and at the air. They
and it, were everywhere, beyond the
lift and the plastic colosseum. (But I
don't tell him that. It's too familiar.)

      *

Anyway, here's the ticket. He takes it
and I am through. My first day
in the city of Brussels!
where nothing will perplex me, I hope.

(It was sort of a plastic thing, out
near the diorama—as I looked at it.)
And nothing does.

Though strangely I am thinking of it,
that plastic thing. You have to laugh:
you take all those big thinkers—Wittgenstein,
Heidegger, Oliver North—and what do they
say the big questions are—*Is you is or is you ain't
my baby?* Stuff like that. No way.

Give me a pigfoot and a bottle of wine, my ticket
and a little umbrella. They're history.

# Wires Crossed Inadvertently

We took the nails out of the day,
tore down the canvas of the sky,
sawed through the chatter of traffic
with a coping saw, before the bees arrived.

Now, upon their arrival we were tired.
We'd done the cutting, the pulling down,
and we'd pulled out all the nails. I hailed them,
tiredly. Bees never speak, they circle,
as they did this day, as if decisively.

The mood was tilting in small shimmering
slats. So we raised its cord with
a thump. A shower of emotional effects
and colored particles. I wanted to take

my wrench to all perspective. The perspective,
everywhere I could see, bent anyway
just after we took out the nails. Clamps
would do it later, we reasoned. A big
G-clamp floated in a vat of molasses

just for that, handy. Then the bees
arrived. We'd done the cutting, the sawing,
the pulling down and were tired. We had
to go, pack everything, and get out of
there quickly. Get a camera on all those
frightened faces, just to see.

The buzz-saw miked. The bee leader,
who was a nutty little guy, small it goes without
saying, but moustachioed in a most amusing
way, with heavy eyebrows, was all for a meeting,
immediately. I was tired. We all were.

Now, and I couldn't believe this, a giant
spinning Fez settled, like at *the end*,
where the credits are still going, the soundtrack
rolls on, a riff—Spanish, or South American—
goes on, a rhythm like the sound of the word "midget"

repeated, repeatedly. Anyway I explained that I was
       tired,
and he said, "Alright. Later."

*from*
# Poems of Relative Unlikelihood

# Proust

Takes me back, this biscuit!

# A Game of Bowls

Ken, this one is the word 'good',
only here it is spelt 'goode'
and, like the others on this grassy patch,
has been sculpted—as you can see—
into a large marble bowling ball.
So have all the others you can see here, around us, as
we walk between them. They also seem like
variants on the word 'good'...
But first, let me explain. I have been looking at
these things for a while now, and I think
this whole 'game' of 'bowls' is a sort of 'text',
that is, it is a text—or several texts—represented graphically
as a gigantic game of bowls. The individual 'balls' are
words, or syntactic links between them, and
their arrangement, here, can be 'read' once you figure
out the rules governing their arrangement.
I also have a sort of intuition that
it is now up to you to set the game into motion. You can do this
by bowling other 'words' at the ones here
or simply by pushing them around with your mind.
You will find, with some practice, that they will
instantly assume the pattern of your thoughts
(or of your will, perhaps).
Okay, so what does this one say? To me, it
looks like a quote from, or partial translation of,
some odd and archaic proverb: "It is goode und gode
that weel is well wode. To dree thee goode wierd."
That's all I can make out. Strange, isn't it? What do you think it
        means?
Wait! You must be thinking now, because the pattern is changing

rapidly.

The game, on the level of a sort of physical and technical
     sub-stratum,
has now been replaced by the one we're entering. That is, by the
pictorial and symbolic level of this play of structured sounds and
     learnt
patterns of meaning and association: in short, of language. (Yet,
     I can
still hear the distant 'clunk' of the earlier 'game' beneath all.)
Well, while we shouldn't forget the obvious interpretations, let's put
these to one side, and also assume there is something mysterious
     going on
here, because the 'text' has started to 'speak' now, saying something
     about
how Paris has been ruined by the Twentieth Century. That is why
     we start
walking through some shuddering, scratched, black and white film—
     Paris of
the 1890s. I don't know about you, but all this makes me angry. It's
     plain
things have changed and I make to shout, "Yes, Paris has been
     ruined by
cars and pollution." But before I do, we arrive at the railway station.
It is mid-day, and there is no train in sight. The 'picture' seems
very naturalistic here. There are twining roses, much art nouveau
     ironwork
on the station balcony, honeysuckle growing in pots—it is a little
     station—
and bees buzzing in the heat. I think to myself, 'Shan (my partner)
     would understand
this place. She likes places like this.' It is so pleasant, that I sleep
     for a
while, on a bench. But when I wake up the scene has changed ...

I have been dreaming—but a dream I am almost
        thankful *to*
rather than for — as though I have visited it, have been
        permitted to. If *you* had gotten
off the train I would have risen, greeted you and we
would have gone to the car and waited for Shan who had been
shopping for a moment, and we would all drive away—Paris
turning into Bega or some country town or the outskirts
of pre-50s Paris—through land that was still used for farming
partly. And if that night we had gone into town
        to the one bar and
talked and drank, having a good time, familiar again,
would we have talked about these things? You are literal,
        cannot invest belief
in symbols, dreams, the irrational, where they present
        themselves
as such. Though you must occasionally find yourself, *after*
        the fact,
to have done so, and it does not worry you then—so it is
        not
that you are against it in principle, but that you are not
        'made' that way.
You talk about railway stations that you can picture,
        sitting on them.
You can see clearly—I can see as I look at you
and you are talking—some geraniums in a dry pot
or tin, painted some colour, green or red. Not
the flowers *I* am seeing—even if you see honeysuckle.
We are close just the same. I am relaxed again,
        glad to be me, glad to be
the age I am. Glad Shan is Shan. I wonder what you are
        doing—
something mundane—putting a record on, say the one you

played for me once you said Sal liked.  If we had gone into town
you might have come back to me—from the phone,
or with more drinks for us—and broken my reverie, saying
'*Hey! Ralphy boy!* last drinks before we go bowling?'—a
reference, via an old TV programme you love (it is
the voice of Art Carney), to the bowling balls,
though I had forgotten them.

# Pedestrian Verse

I walked down to the corner of my street
and turned where the bunting swayed, listless
a little. *Then they kicked up!* a breeze moved them.

The footpath had been chewed a bit,
to widen it,
by a tractor at one end.

Near the garage were a lot of little lights,
but it was daylight and they weren't on.

I took a note from my wallet,
put it in my left shirt pocket then
in my pants, then back in my wallet again.

A nervous habit. I felt then
where it no longer was.
I do these things.

Feeling for it still now, with some urgency,
I had it in my hand as I approached
the counter of the petrol station—which doubles

where I live as a food and grocery store—
bought a stick of chocolate that I had
never tried on any afternoon prior to this

simply on a whim.

The girls at the bus stop chewed and stared,
stared and chewed, and one of them said
"What's the time?  When's the bus coming?"

I said, *I don't know. I'm from out of town—I know nothing
of what goes on around here.*
I often do this.

It makes me feel young, because irresponsible,
or so I think.

I went round the block,
the bigger block, not the little one,
as I really wanted to walk.

I thought about what the girls had said.

Or the way they had said it.  They had
addressed me
out of some slight curiosity.  I wondered what I had done

to deserve it.  I hummed a little song—"Tomato time,
tomato time"—to a Latin American rhythm, but I could
think over the top of it, as it was unobtrusive,

in fact
it kept time with how I walked.

But once I rounded the corner
away from the girls' gaze
my walk slowed and I gradually began, though I didn't
        notice,

to abandon the song.
"Abandon"—
heavy word.

Anyway, I saw a number of uninteresting things,
but this simply causes me to think, become more inward—
or irritated if I am tired.

One does, then,
blame the itinerary,
and think of it as tiresome.

On a day such as this, though, I did not
think it tiresome.  As streets go, it is a familiar
and quite interesting street.  That is why I walk it.

# Air

What is tangible beyond the air
seems a promise, merely, beyond the air's
own tangibility. A promise we hold back
from proving, the air seems so tangible.
Solid air, in which all your hopes
now are, immanent, bright, but also,
quick to displace one another, like children asked
to volunteer for something, who mill about
giggling, You go first, you go first. No, you. Nothing devolves
from this ether, as if you could give back to the air
the grace your attention precludes from being
here. Something perceived become prayer.

# Twins I

These guys making hamburgers all night
Don't look like twins to me.
You look up at the moon
And suddenly
Are calmer.  You can sigh,
Accept sadness, and shoulder it on
Into the future, and also eat your burger.

# Twins II

These guys making hamburgers all night
don't look like twins
though that's what the sign says,
outside, at four a.m.:  TWINS.
You look at them.
The guy beside you does it too,
figuring it out.
You walk away,
to different cars,
same idea in your heads,
same hamburger in your hands.
Twins.

# After Lunch Hour

Curious green marching of the aphids' feet upon the rose.

They are curious—but they are curious in their own right,
and I do not like to compare them to things.

*"The century opens its big wooden door."* That
is better. This is not serious—a relief—and
not particular. No responsibility—
no hope either.

The most ordinary thought in your own head
is better than the best thought in another's—
the poet Jamie Grant said, in consideration of
authenticity. Oh well, back to the kennels.

I look in, to see if the animals are clean,
have water and etcetera. Above the city
are aeroplanes. There are eight lifts
that all go up. Only one
goes to the basement. I take that lift.

Here I am with the angora pellets.

I take a bag and catch the lift back up.
The polished stone and glass round the lift-well,
misted by steam from the zoo's canteen,
betrays the century's promise—modernity,
clean lines, a softened functionalism. You walk
out again to the cages, a pocket full of greens.
"I'm," you sing, "going catch the yak train,

Yak train—yak train to Gibraltar,"
to the tune of *'A' Train*, and you feed them them.

# Midas: from a Kitchen Window

I look down upon the world
from my cloud and pool setting, down onto the sad highway
below.
They are another order,

if this is order.

Beyond my great industrial parks
I see the tired
people of the world, envious of the blue desks of clerks
of accountants pulling at the cistern—
I see them streaming, hurrying to their perks
or lack of them, all in vain turmoil striving.

I cling to blind determinism,
and go on living here, above the dross,
where there are no 'things', only processes—

go on living like they do
and turn on my golden vats,
in the warming darkness.

# Who Left Out the Washing?

These guys aint so tough: Cause they always blame
everything on women—the crummy sets,
the plastic boulders, bad lighting on the dragon,
bad electricals on the dragon (eyes won't work—
they should light up) an idea
a maggot could of thought of, frankly!  They
keep pointing over their shoulder & saying,
"She did it!"  If this movie don't come in on time,
says one, taint my fault.  Nah,
"she did it," says the other, sittin' in their
trailer van, watching, as the rain comes down, occasionally
trying to tune the radio.  Even the fuckin radios
don't work round here!
*And whose job was it*
to bring in the washing?!

# Which One!

Heem.

# Sandwich Hand

My hands are like a sandwich,
the right one ham, ham-fisted,
out the sides poke little bits of lettuce.
The left is more primitive—

globs of clotted gore
over a bone
to hit you with, like a club.

All day outside the stadium,
with the Dippy Dog and waffle vans,
waiting for the end of the big game,

the striped tigers and rare pangolin
that you'll only see
in old *National Geographics*.
(If at all.)

We have ated them, me and the crowds,
ated them all up, my little personburger.

I have watched you.  You are sexy,
but you are edible.  I am a higher order.
All day long I tend you, my flock, feed you sadly—
burger, sammitch, sauce and gerkins,

which I hand you in a little bag,
wrapped in a handtowel that is tiny
but means a lot—a reference to that sphere we dream of
you, me, everyone on this planet—life in the palace,
      the casino, the resort,


where I am tended by houris,
who look like you, admittedly, and I feed them,
but I don't *have* to feed them:
you love me, and I am not a sandwich hand.

*from*
Nutters Without Fetters

# The God of Trieste, Arezzo, Adelaide, Pisa, Leipzig and Other Smaller Cities Looks Down

Sometimes I look out on all the hopeless crud
that's going down in this town
and watch the small figures walk below,
about their business
—which is only penny ante
according to some god-like position, which,
admittedly, is literally mine.
But it's best to get some perspective on this—
it's only a little town, Trieste (so are
Arezzo and Adelaide, and Leipzig—the towns
I look after). A figure
wanders by the river, head in the clouds
daydreaming and I feel 'fond', maybe, but not
                    involved
and I do not watch its progress. But the figure,
her shoulders forward, walking too quickly,
and absorbedly, by that same river—
the Arno if it is Pisa, the Torrens if Adelaide—
then I care. Her trouble seems so great,
unknown to me, and the setting
too ridiculous, too kooky
as backdrop—for any human drama.

But they can't see this.

I, of course, can't see it from their perspective!
Down amongst it, surrounded
by it, the river seems real enough; tears

blurring the ridiculous architecture.  It's
this mystery I cannot know:
her so evident suffering, his agony of indecision,
sense of worthlessness, the child's despair
and resignation, and its miniature quality,
that blinds the tiny figure
to the bland but amusing beauties of the city.
I do not understand how they feel—
What troubles them?

   The serene, the
happy, the delirious figure
sees things as I do: small, the city about them
provides security, is niche, is bower, is a pedestal perhaps,
   a dispensation.

I see them the same way.

Of course I cannot see myself.
I am aware of myself—true—but not so that I gain
or attain, if even only briefly, higher ground:
I am up here looking down.  I know
that I am happy and involved in the lives below,
my city, when the traffic flows and the day goes on
and small figures here and there are preoccupied
         in their Lilliputian
but dear way.  Their emotions colour the city.
The distressed rider—curious statue
outside their parliament—seems tragic,
emblem of the heightened state they feel, and its inadequacy
gives a kind of pathos: the buses
with their red noses on 'Red Nose Day' for instance—
bathetic.  And I care more than I can say

and can do nothing.  It is my all day study
and my midnight dream, to see that same figure emerge
and to follow it the next day, sadly weaving through

                                  the streets,

carrying, trailing its troubles.  Are they the same?
Worse, or different?  What will make them 'go away'?

Or I am bored—I am not needed here,
no one is troubled, things run smoothly.  The town
is only a town, people have their place in it.
What am I doing up here in these spires, the traffic going by
soundlessly almost?  I am bored.

But take that man openning up that bar-and-pizzeria—
I have seen him before.  He is troubled.  What
ails him?  See how he pauses with the key?
And then he opens it!  Finally.  And at
the same bar—which looks pleasant enough
(he is switching on the neon sign now—see, it
flickers a little faultily most nights, for the first few hours,
a beautiful green and red and blue and white that I think
was once yellow but has faded)—the young woman,
here she comes now, she always comes at just this time,
is strangely troubled too.  She has been for days.  I cannot
get over it.
                Oh, these dreadful pigeons!

Where is the life for me, that I can worry about?
Why don't the mountains beckon, the distant hills,
they should, but they never do.

# 5 Paintings

— expatriate poems —

notes from our Grand Tour

# "Cinque minuta!"

They went naked into battle, pure form, without
faces, and you have painted them as at a barbeque.
To the left ancient columns echo
the gasometer, which rises beyond one marble
      shoulder
to the right, & on which it leans, a
friendly gasometer. A noble business, requiring
very long faces. Your design is adequate: their faces
are longer than commuters', who have missed a train,
& stand on the Flinders Street Station, mortified—
      dinner
will be burned or cold—though the white horse rears,
a still shell shape in the distance, & the bold youth
cannot be restrained. Yet all softens
in pigments, like regret, or the ideal of silence
lost in sunlight. Five minutes
& we must leave the gallery, painting by de Chirico.
I will go home & have dinner.

# Bernini

St. Theresa's heresy was to say
that if there is a soul, it is pure,
at one with God, unstainable in spite of
our sins, beyond words & deeds.  It can't be
changed.  If stone were liquid this might breathe.
St. Theresa breathes—a last breath, uninterrupted
which goes on: time, the curvature of resolution,
the fruition of completion, involve a taint & corruption
unallowable to her.  Where Cupid dandles
a burning tip Bernini jokes mildly, affectionately,
with the possibility of her belief
& she inhabits the endless space of her ecstasy.

To think that this was structural!
He was a great architect, almost nothing built—
his desires, too, unnameable as
bricks or mortar.

# Frans Hals

Yes, that they were flawed, human, even
a little ridiculous, but mostly that they were like
you & me; & the faces flushed, as if
begging the question of your sympathy.
He liked to drink, I guess. And that was
a weakness & a boast. I drink too,
actually. And yet if you enter their
attention & not your own, they do
beg the question: Here am I & here
are you. The portrait, *Willem Van Heythuysen*
has him teeter on his chair. I don't like him. I
don't feel that he especially likes me either, or
would like me. As he aged he became
more essential, his earlier works more popular
in their time. It is only recently that the severe
paintings have gained approval. His honesty
was a burden that shrank his palette. In their costumes,
their tiny social stratifications make them hard to like—
so much rectitude displayed in self-defence. One likes
the earlier sitters best, & the later paintings.
He was a master of the monotone,
      his defeat
by the truth, which he told however.

# Max Ernsts

When I went into the Peggy Guggenheim in
Venice I saw some of them there, Max Ernsts.
Very pretty, more than you would've expected.
The radiance prior to thought burned there,
the void from which ideas are born irradiated her
face, as if from an impossible distance, yet her fur
could not contain its lightning. That is
how it struck me. But I like surrealism. I respond
to it too sympathetically, quiver too much in pitch
with its leanings. Max Ernst knocked me sideways,
in the gentlest possible ways. Yes, we really are poets
& the little vaporettos (boats that go along the grand
canal) towed a rich woman's toys along the grand
   canal.

# Beckmann

Everyone admires the muscular strength
with which you enforce the terms of the proofs
& demonstrations that are your paintings.
Lessons from a hard master.  You crumpled up
Roualt like a stained glass window in
a car compressor.  All that space he wasted,
that easy & slight asymmetry you turn
to just proportion & a cruel accounting.  I
think we like you for the wrong reasons,
but we will never like Roualt so much again.
Whipping boy on your hobby horse—always
the same one—daddy & mummy, & puss 'n boots,
the nurse with her duelling scar.  This belongs on
          television.
Our approval is the beginning of your welcome there.
But you are gone.
                    Little Jesus in the tin hat
rehearsing claustrophobia & masturbation.
Scary, scary, scary.

# Böcklin

You go windswept to that island, little figure,
your cloak shaped like a sarcophagus,
      an Egyptian one,
as befits your late 19th century period's enthusiasms.
It is hard not to feel for you.  Anyway, there you
go, standing in the boat like that.  Good,
      that you never
get there, & stand with your back to us, we get
to look just a little over your shoulder & so to ask
you the question.  And if we know not what the
question is, too bad, too dumb of *us* is
      the implication,
you romantic little blighter.

# Nutter Thing

Pappy, I priv-el-ege my chicken
coop, fer'n it's art to me,
Lands! Aigs 'n all, roosters settin'
purty as pigfat on rashers.  I
privaleges that coop!  Fore-ground it too.
Now why is that?  Tell yer why:
oncet, aged three, or four—
or thereabouts—little anyway,
out in the yard, I had this dream:
caused by I stood on the rake's pointy ending
& it swung up 'n hit me.  Bonk!
Like to have divided my brain
(reason, Jed says, I'm so pernicketty *now*—
other times I got what that
baiter of bears called
"negative capability".  I black out
&, after a few seconds tick past,
a pinhole of light happens
gits wider gradually—*very* gradual—
& then I hear the birds & chickens
& stuff, maybe the dog's barkin', or
a plane's flyin' by overhead & the pinpoint of light
is wide & is the whole day & I'm
a-lookin' up & the dog's lickin' me
on the face & Jed, or one of the kids,
is sayin' Nan, get up.  And I do—
I go about my day!)  Well, once
*this* happened: I passed out
& woke thinkin' some giant bird
was towerin' above,

its angry, wrathful eye & beak about
to land like a guillotine
on poor helpless me, or, like Sinbad,
pick me up & fly away.  But it was
just a faint & it was just a chicken
standin' there, on my chest, probably thinkin'
why had I stopped feedin'?—who knows
what chickens think?  I think they *don't* think
most days—& up I gets, & ever since
(& I was only eleven—did I say three?  three then!)
I had a beard & this yen to be an artist.
Little scene inside I made outa matchsticks 'n
                    thistles—
depicts John Wilkes Booth murderin' Abe Lincoln—
with the stage & curtains & actors & the rest of the
                    audience,
horror on their little faces & the gleam on Booth's
                              eye.
Miracle.  Like the cruelty in the eye of that chicken.

*from*
Lucky For Some

# Volatile Condensate

My dream once for the north wing of the building—
a vast mural of Fred and Wilma done
'after Poussin'—is on hold.  Unregretted.

What do you say to Jackson Pollock in a lift?
Obviously, the numbers climb higher and higher,
and expensive graffiti gets pulled out of the wall

at midnight, and carted away on a truck.  You say
*Que sera, sera* and duck.  Straightening up, slowly,
I explain my other dream to him: Gericault's portrait

of the back of Delacroix's head in old age.
Jackson laughs—"Like mine of Bill de Kooning
aged ninety!" he says.  Downstairs we throw the spray cans on
        the fire and watch them explode.

# Never Mr Beep

You get to wear the flipper feet.  But so what?  Every
clown can do that, the slap-walk.  And the flower squirter
in your button hole, for the front row.  But
driving the funny car, I never get that.  No, Never Mr Beep,

though with my name I was born for it.  Wasn't I?  I look out
through the rain at the marshland and reeds, & the ducks.
Could you cull them?  But think of the noise, all the blood.
You could do it chemically?  But I am not that kind of creep.  Surely.

Tooting, I ride the unicycle straight up
the cliff top, topple slightly, back and forth and breathe the sea air in—
never miss a beat.  I miss one this time, flip around,
hurtle down the hill again.  The horn on this thing works I think.

# Headlines Above a Woman's Face

In the portrait of *'Lil, as a bacchante—Sal's place,*
*Elizabeth Bay'*—coffee cup, garden seat, at the left, and
on the right, the face—'the law of the excluded middle'
adequately named the middle ground.

A jet pencilled vapour across the sky.
She looked up, and the whole day shook slightly.
The profile seemed back-lit, almost heroic,
against the moment I described, but darkness

flooding fast from the edges of the day, just intensifying the island
of clarity at its centre, her gaze: which seemed, curiously,
fixed upon a bungled bust of Beethoven—and a picture of Sartre,
    Wilma,
and the Simones, de Beauvoir and Signoret.

# (CWP) Centurion Wheelchair Pallor

is a rare condition, becoming more common, unfortunately.
It's the chair, and the patient (client, punter, stooge, whatever).
The chair because the brakes fail pretty regularly: a hill, a

flight of stairs… You can imagine. There is also "the indisputable fact"
(in the phrase of my idiot co-worker, nurse Merle Doder),
these people aren't so fit anymore—and are "unfitter increasingly"

(to quote her again): The Puff Factor.
"Trouble with the past, is it's over. The future,
you never get to it. And I don't have time for now.

There's a skate-boarder I run with. He lets me beat
him over the speed humps sometimes. Realia gets in
the way. Then the staff come and get me for lunch."

# The Problem of Other Minds
*two uncollected poems*

# Unconditioned Weirdness

Who's a nutter? (Un-
answerable, of course.)

But, *how everything is so conjoined,*
I love it!

Phenomena.
All of which must bear scrutiny.
If we are to know them, and love them
as themselves, not just an instance
of our personal weird,
but as the weird itself.

This is a tricky thing to do. Many
don't approach it.


These things are the trust they must place in us.
For this we came, & stand here on our own two feet,
   nuttilly albeit.

    "A place in the sun,
     A place in the shade."


"I guess you see things differently."

# Just a Thought

It's my birthday
and the pajamas hang on a hook
the pajamas of another birthday
and they mark a continuity,

It makes me think of the yesterdays
I wasn't here.

I do not have to think this thing.

It is the emptiness of the pajamas. But
'Back to bed?' No way!

There's a river behind the drive-in
where I floated tin cans as a kid—
not a river really
sort of the wash-off from the locale's industry.

I feel like going there, but I feel like
going in my pajamas. *That*
is out of the question.

This thought occurred to me then.
You could almost cut it with a knife—
one for the books.
Like a rubber glove caught in a pinball machine
stretching me sideways and all yelling to stop:
It was this—That *wherever I might go*
in my chequered lapels, no day
would be the same as this.

On the other hand, I could go back to bed and
no day would be the same either!

All happened, and happened upon.
The primary locust and tertiary forge,
The daydream after dinner, the furious cycle ...
(*If* you take my meaning.)

These thoughts I have.

Ken Bolton & John Jenkins have been writing collaboratively since the middle 80s though their friendship goes back to mid-70s Sydney. The poems were composed while the authors were together, laughing, frowning, hitting each other on the head with rolled-up newspapers, and via a mix of procedures: talking at cross-purposes, insidious undermining, go-you-one-betterism, you-do-the-ideas-I'll-do-the-afterthought-&-description. Or, I'll say the things you'd say—you say the things I'd say. And finally, Look, this-thing-needs-finishing—and sundry other methods.

Individually the authors have numerous books to their credit. Yet their co-written works hold a special place in the hearts of all. Yes, all.

www.ingramcontent.com/pod-product-compliance
Lightning Source LLC
Chambersburg PA
CBHW030943090426
42737CB00007B/516